VISUAL GRAMMAR: DESIGN FOUNDATIONS FOR EDITORS

BY
KRISTY S. GILBERT

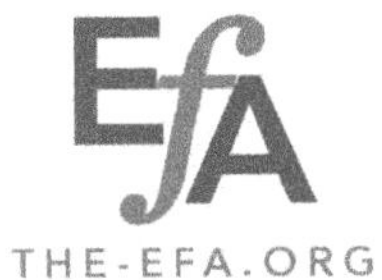

266 West 37th St. 20th Floor
New York, NY 10018
office@the-efa.org

ISBN paperback 978-1-880407-50-9
ISBN ebook 978-1-880407-51-6

Gilbert, Kristy S. *Visual Grammar: Design Foundations for Editors.*
Published in the United States of America by the Editorial Freelancers Association.

BISAC Subject Categories: Design/Book | Design/Graphic Arts/General | Language Arts & Disciplines/Publishers & Publishing Industry

Legal Disclaimer

While the publisher and author have made every attempt to verify that the information provided in this book is correct and up to date, the publisher and author assume no responsibility for any error, inaccuracy, or omission. The advice, examples, and strategies contained herein are not suitable for every situation. Neither the publisher nor author shall be liable for damages arising therefrom. This book is not intended for use as a source of legal or financial advice. Running a business involves complex legal and financial issues. You should always retain competent legal and financial professionals to provide guidance.

EFA Publications Director: Robin Martin
Copyeditor: Monica White
Proofreader: Ebonye Gussine Wilkins
Book Designer: Kevin Callahan | BNGO Books
Cover Designer: Ann Marie Manca

See more by the author:

LooseleafEP.com
BestBookTemplates.com

Contents

Visual Grammar: Design Foundations for Editors

Most editors know the ins and outs of written rhetoric. They can adjust for emphasis, organization, and clarity by choosing a synonym with different connotations, shifting a clause, or trimming a paragraph. But when it comes to achieving the same effects with visual rhetoric, some editors feel out of their depth.

Design awareness is becoming increasingly important in publishing models embraced by businesses, web publishers, and rapid release book publishers. As models that emphasize quickly reaching readers and customers often cut down on the number of trained professionals who touch a piece before it publishes or goes live, editors of all stripes become more valuable in these production chains if they understand the basic grammar of document design. Personally, I market myself as a book editor and designer, and I've seen how bundling editing and design services appeals to clients and improves my bottom line.

Like editing, visual design isn't about hard-and-fast rules. It's about styling layouts in ways that help a project's message reach its intended audience. Each design benefits from specific choices based on foundational graphic design principles, which provide rhetorical tools to help organize, emphasize, and clarify texts in ways that are appropriate for a finalized, ready-to-publish work.

There are up to a dozen foundational principles, but arguably the most important of them are **contrast**, **repetition**, **alignment**, and **proximity**. Armed with an understanding of these principles, you can use visual grammar to create a coherent hierarchy of information for readers and viewers. Once you've structured your documents well, you can fine-tune the typefaces and typesetting to create elegant and effective reader-ready documents.

Foundations of Good Design

Four core principles at the foundation of design awareness are contrast, repetition, alignment, and proximity. Think of them as the visual grammar equivalent of parts of speech. Designers can use all of them in different ways to create flow, cohesion, and readability. These principles don't cover all the tools designers use, but they're a good place to start for functional design. In prose terms, these aren't how you write the next Great American Novel, but they will help you turn in a set of usable technical directions.

These principles also aren't fully independent of each other. No single principle creates a stunning design all by itself, and some principles are more important for one type of design than another. But if you're setting up a new design or trying to diagnose one that looks off, it can be helpful to sit with each principle and examine how the design implements it.

Contrast

Contrast is a principle that covers all the ways in which elements of a design are different, and it is best used to create emphasis. Editors run into this principle all the time. In basic running text, most of the type looks the same, but if *one* word is put in a *different* type style, it creates *emphasis*. Italics, when applied to just a few words in a passage of roman type, change the way a reader approaches those words. This is the principle of contrast at work. You can create contrast with just about any visual element of a design—read on for a few more of these methods.

Size

Most people realize that they can make something stand out on a page by making it bigger than everything else on the page. But making something big isn't the only way to create contrast. Contrast is all about difference. If most of the elements in a design are a similar size, then whichever element deviates from that size stands out. For example, if a series of dots are all a medium size, then either a large or a small dot can draw a viewer's eye first because it breaks the pattern.

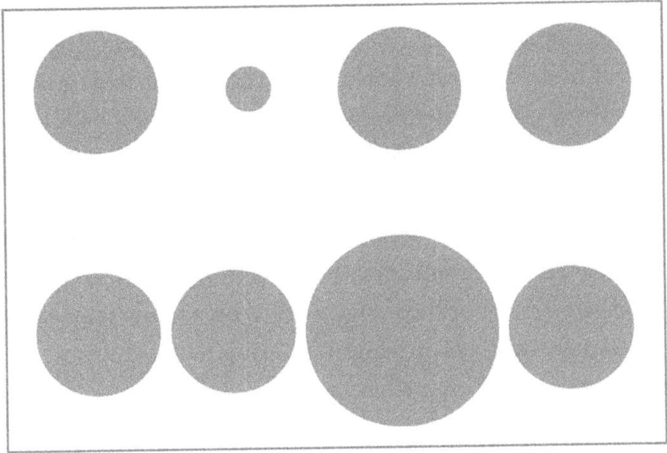

Figure 1. In each line of dots, the different dot is the one that stands out.

This works with text as well as with shapes. Of course large text stands out if most of the text around it is small. But if most of the text on a flyer is large—perhaps so big that the letters become decorative elements more than legible words—then small text stands out.

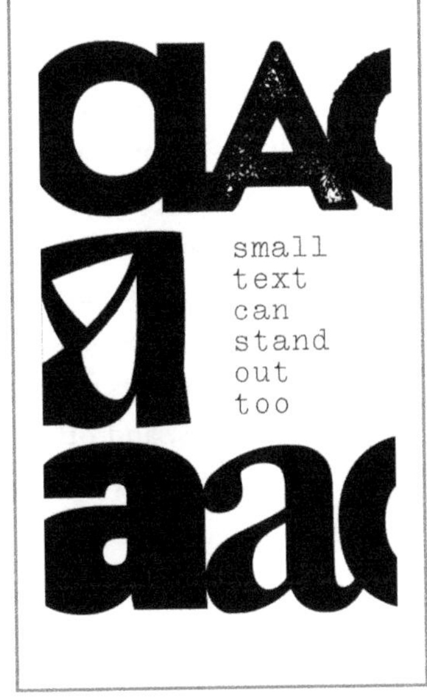

Figure 2. The small text stands out in a sea of oversized As. Fonts used: P22 Specimen (the small text); Queulat Black, Brandon Printed, Chalif Rough, Trickster, Acumin UltraBlack, and Adobe Caslon Pro Bold (the various As).

More subtle size contrast can also communicate differences between groups of text. For example, captions are often smaller than regular running text—it's part of how designers signal that captions are separate.

Color & Value

Color contrast is a difference in hue, like blue and orange. Value contrast is a difference in shade, like a very pale and very dark version of royal blue. Both color and value serve as sources for contrast.

If you're working with a medium that permits more colors—like full-color printing or design for screens—a limited palette of accent colors is a powerful tool. Pick out a selection of colors that look good together and deploy those colors intentionally. Warm colors (like red, orange, and yellow) often seem to come forward in a design, and cool colors (like blue, green, and purple) often recede into the background.

But even in black-and-white designs, color contrast—in the form of value contrast—is important. For example, a light gray box with text in it will stand out if most of the design's text is on a white page. A dark gray or black box (probably with white text inside) would create even more contrast in a document on a white page.

Typeface (or Font)

Typefaces (or fonts) can also create strong contrast. Documents rarely change typefaces in the middle of a paragraph, but contrasting typefaces can help titles, headings, call-out boxes, and decorative text elements stand out from a document's basic running text.

The key with type contrast is to be bold about it (and I don't mean always using bolded text). Using fonts that are too similar reduces the impact of your design. The differences between Times New Roman and Garamond (the body text typeface for this book), for example, are significant enough to notice, but not significant enough to look like switching between them is a purposeful choice. Both typefaces have serifs (the little lines at the top and bottom of most letter stems), average stroke thickness, and other elements that make them reliable choices for body text. They don't make a good contrasting pair.

For strong type contrast, two good rules of thumb are (1) to stick to one to three typefaces per design and (2) to choose typefaces from different basic type categories: serif, sans serif, slab serif, and decorative.

Serif typefaces have serifs (little lines at the top and bottom of many letter stems). Because serif fonts are, in American publishing, traditional for books and other printed materials, designers often choose serif fonts for book body text, magazine and newspaper articles, and websites that have longer and more in-depth articles. Some common examples are Times New Roman, Garamond, and Georgia.

Sans serif typefaces have no serifs. This omission often makes their letterforms simpler and easier to read quickly. Sans serifs are the most commonly used type category for body text online. Some common examples are Helvetica, Arial, Calibri, and Verdana.

Slab serif typefaces have thick, blocky serifs. While there are some slab serifs appropriate for body text (Chaparral, for example), they are usually better suited for larger sizes where it's appropriate for type to have a louder personality. Some common slab serifs are Rockwell, Courier, and Joanna.

Decorative typefaces don't neatly fit into the other categories. They include fonts that mimic handwriting or calligraphy—like cursive or blackletter fonts—and also serif, sans serif, and slab serif fonts that emphasize decorative elements over stately readability.

If you pick only one to three typefaces and ensure each is from a separate category, you'll likely create strong type contrast. For example, a serif body text paired with a sans serif heading font is a classic and effective combination.

Font Style & Case

Some designs are better served by sticking to a single font family. (This can cut down on font licensing costs and create unified branding.) If you're working within a single font family, you still have type contrast options.

Many font families have italic and bold versions, and some font families have an even wider selection of font weights (these versions usually range from *light* or *thin* to *extrabold* or *black*). These font styles provide a range of contrast options from within the same font family.

Acumin Thin

Acumin Thin Italic

Acumin Extra Light

Acumin Extra Light Italic

Acumin Light

Acumin Light Italic

Acumin Regular

Acumin Italic

Acumin Medium

Acumin Semibold

Acumin Bold

Acumin Black

Acumin Ultra Black

Figure 3. Acumin Pro comes in a variety of weights, and each weight also comes with its own italic. Not all families are this robust; some come in only one weight or lack true italics.

Type case can create contrast just as strong. ALL CAPS text creates emphasis when it's surrounded by sentence case or lowercase text. Two levels of heading could have the same typeface, font weight, and size, but if one is in all caps and another in title case, readers will know the headings mean different things.

Alignment

Alignment is a foundational principle of its own (as we'll see later), but designers can also use it to create contrast. Alignment contrast is a way to arrange elements of a design to indicate that they're distinct from each other. An easy example of this is a title that is centered above body text that is left-aligned. Alignment contrast is also what makes block quotes stand out as different from regular running text—block quotes are indented more deeply than regular body text. Even though the block quotes are left-aligned (or "flush left"), they line up with a different vertical line than the running text. That different placement sends a visual signal that emphasizes the block quote, so readers know they're quotes rather than the author's original words.

Example

Figure 4 is an example of the first page of a lead magnet that has several design elements: a document title, an image, a caption, two different heading levels, a decorative pull quote, and running text.

The title—the first thing the designer wants the reader to see—is in big, bold 26-point font and has a different background than every other element, one of solid black (which contrasts about as strongly as possible on a white page). To maximize legibility, the text is white, which contrasts with the dark background.

The first-level heading is in a sans serif font (while the body text is in a serif font), is set in all caps, and is set at 16 points (the regular text is 11 points). These contrasting elements guide readers who are skimming through the document for the main sections.

The second-level heading needs to be different from the body text, so it's also in a sans serif font. But it doesn't need to stand out as much as the first-level heading because it's less important, so it's only 14 points tall and is set in title case rather than all caps.

This Is a Lead Magnet

HEADING LEVEL 1

Sit et odi volupti consed eum quas magnimus, cum, nisquas sed milibus archit, illenis vollore aditias rent vendam nam, aut que voles am rae veniminicit as es il mod expe ratibus cillatem. Pudanimi, que volor alibusae dolorem id quam reicid es porit occum que nesenditat audi qui assitis quoditis sinis eatis re.

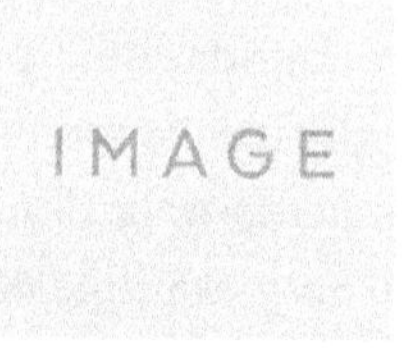

This caption is smaller and aligned differently than the running text.

Quatiusciae con nonsequati rent, sequis abo. Nequia consequos aliste audisque poritetur aborporro etur sum inctess enditia sum et harcips anditiuria prenditi omnis etur, sinum etur sumet, tentem rest ut omnia quam serci doloriam aut rerae es quidistis aut postium earchicium eum et occus etur? Non et, tem ipsae dolorit expliqu ametur?

Heading Level 2

Itatur sum quo berem eium, conse ne volores cipsam quassimpere dolupta volupic tem simperibus eum et et modit, volupta venime.

This decorative pull quote is large and in a typeface from a different category.

Laborup taeperum voluptatem nimolenia dolore rerecum etumeni hitaquam nullam illorporia amenis maximporrum rempore mosam quodi aut facest optatur?

Figure 4. A sample lead magnet page. Fonts used: Eldwin Script Regular, Texta Regular, and Minion Pro Regular & Italic.

The caption, while set in the same typeface, differs from the running text in that it is smaller, set in italics, and right-aligned. So even though the caption is embedded in the running text, readers can tell it's meant to be something different.

The pull quote also needs to be different from the running text. Since it's mostly decorative, it uses the script font from the title rather than the body text font, is set in a larger size, and is center-aligned.

These style choices guide the reader through the message in a way that flows and is not overwhelming. Instead of using an intimidating block of text, the message is divided into smaller, more digestible chunks. By emphasizing (or downplaying) certain parts, the design leads readers' focus and gets the message across in a way that serves the design's purpose.

Contrast Misfires

If you have a design that isn't quite clicking and you're not sure why, examine the contrast between different design elements. The two most common mistakes designers make with contrast are being too timid with it or conversely, overusing it without a purpose.

With timid contrast, you can always be braver. If you have different levels of headings but they're not very clear, put the higher-level heading in all caps, make it bold, or add some other element of contrast. If some words are too hard to read on a given background, increase the color contrast between the words and the background. If two typefaces aren't quite doing the trick, consider using different, more contrasting typefaces.

Purposeless contrast is the opposite problem. It's contrast that doesn't intentionally guide the reader's eye. Think of purposeless contrast like filler words in an overstuffed sentence: Ditch it! If you're designing a quarterly business report and it's full of zany colors that distract from the data, tone it down and scale back the color scheme to a more limited palette. Purposeless contrast may look more exciting, but it can also undermine how effectively a design communicates.

Repetition

On the other end of the spectrum is **repetition**. Repetition covers all the ways in which elements in a design appear more than once, and it's best used for creating clarity. You can repeat the same things you use to create contrast—size, color, typeface, and all the rest are candidates for repetition.

When a designer employs the same typeface for all the body paragraphs in a document, the reader understands those paragraphs are part of the main text. When all the block quotes have the same indentation, readers clearly see they are all the same sort of thing: long quotes embedded in the main flow of the text.

Repetition is the concept most editors have the easiest time with. Many of us spend our days ferreting out inconsistencies and standardizing writing to style guides and language guidelines. Visual repetition is simply a different sort of consistency.

Color

Many editors I work with approach color as a decorative element and think of it mostly in terms of contrast. It stands out and adds pizzazz! But color is also a powerful tool of repetition. Repeating a color at different points in a design can guide a viewer's eye from one instance of that color to the next.

Repeating a color can direct the viewer's focus and create rhythm and unity. If the same color appears at the top and bottom of a design and a couple other places in between, it guides the viewer top-to-bottom. For example, the simple infographic in Figure 5 uses the same dark gray as the background color for the top and bottom bars, for the headings for each data set, and for the cut-out piece of the pie chart.

Repeating this color implies the order in which the designer wants the viewer to see the information and maintains consistency throughout the design. Designers can achieve similar effects with accent colors on book covers, in heading levels, and more.

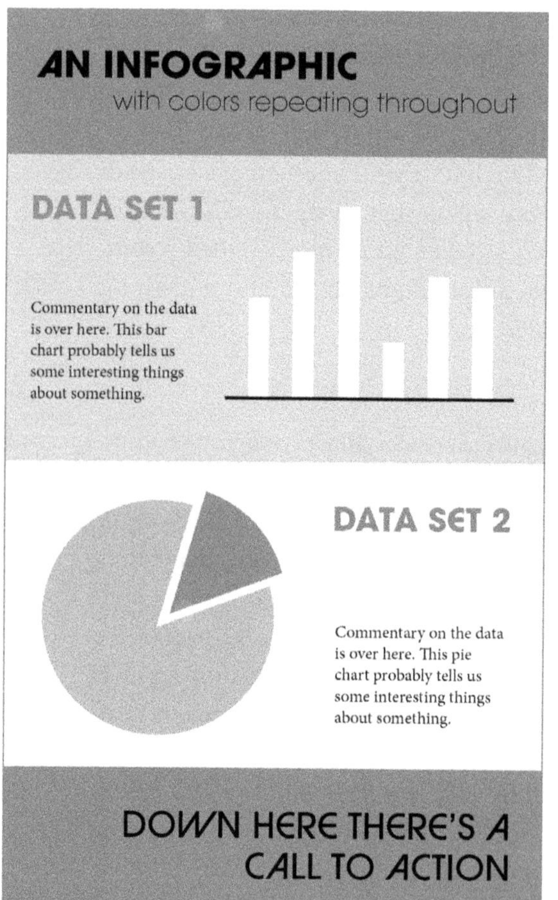

Figure 5. Fonts used: ITC Avant Garde Gothic (various weights) and Minion Pro Regular.

Brand Style

Repetition is also a powerful strategy to create clarity and unity across a variety of documents and visuals that belong together. Just as companies and publications have style guides for their text, many also have style guides for their visuals—pamphlets, online ads, flyers, social media graphics, reports, and more. These branding style guides make it easy to ensure consistency in fonts, colors, and other elements repeated across their marketing material.

Editorial freelancers often design their own documents and graphics as needed for their businesses. A consistent visual style guide can create a unified, coherent visual experience no matter where your clients interact with you. For example, for my company's designs I rely heavily on Texta, a robust sans serif font family I use for titles, headings, and text. I put most headings in all caps. I have a color palette of grays, greens, and an aqua blue that I use as often as possible in my business-related designs (letterhead, website, handouts, etc.). This gives my company a unified visual style and—bonus!—I don't have to come up with design features from scratch every time I need a new graphic. Repetition doesn't just clarify; it relieves some of the mental strain of designing.

Repetition Misfires

If you're diagnosing a design that isn't working, check to see if you have the right amount of repetition to bring your design together. A long book will need more repetition than a music festival poster, so keep your audience, purpose, and message in mind.

If the design looks too scattered or your test viewers have a hard time figuring out where to look with all the different elements, change some the elements' styles to match each other. Use fewer colors, align things more uniformly, or ditch one of your decorative typefaces. Create cohesiveness by employing fewer styles and consistency by echoing them strategically across your design. To make both sides of a business card look like they belong together, repeat some element on both sides—a shape, a color, a font, etc.

Conversely, if it's difficult to tell that a design has distinct elements—headings, captions, etc.—then it might have too much repetition. When a design presents elements that serve very different purposes but use the same type size and other style features, the design gets muddy. Add some contrast to emphasize focal points and important elements!

Alignment

Alignment dictates how elements of a design line up with each other, both vertically and horizontally. Good alignment guides readers' eyes to flow up and down or left and right across a design, which means it's an excellent tool for organizing information.

For the purposes of this booklet, I discuss alignment in the context of designing for an audience primarily made up of folks who read left-to-right and top-to-bottom. This sort of audience naturally starts at the top left corner of a design unless a designer does something dramatic to encourage them to look elsewhere. (Alignment works similarly for other audiences, but those audiences look to other parts of a design first.)

Vertical Alignment

For most documents, the main two types of vertical alignment designers use are center and left. Center alignment creates balance, but the tradeoff is that it often creates weaker guiding lines going up and down a design because centered elements often begin and end at different places on the page. Left- or right-aligned elements share at least one clean line going vertically, so these styles create better guiding lines. Although they may not look as balanced as center-aligned elements, they often create an asymmetry that attracts and guides eyeballs.

Smartphone text message threads use alignment to organize different elements and guide viewers' eyes. In a message thread between two people, Person 1's text boxes are all aligned to the

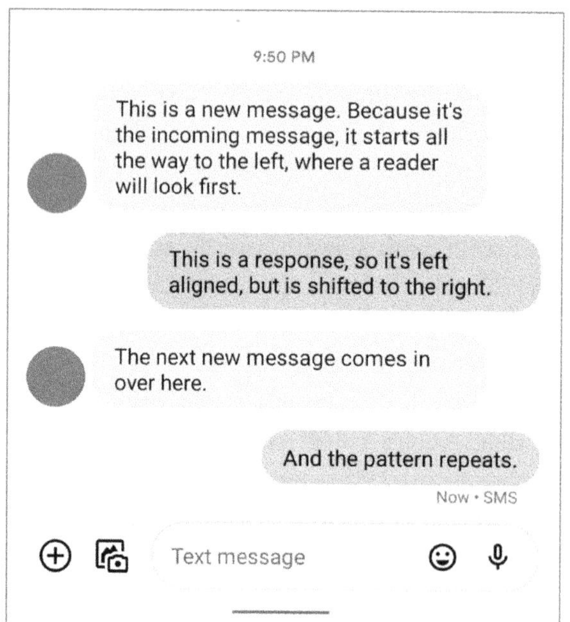

Figure 6. Text message apps typically use alignment to organize messages by sender.

far left of the screen. Person 2's text boxes are aligned along the right side of the screen. (The *text* of Person 2's messages is still left-aligned—left-aligned text is easiest to read—but the boxes containing the text are flush right.)

The alignment for all of Person 1's text boxes is repeated; the alignment for all of Person 2's text boxes is repeated. But different alignments make it easy to know who wrote each message, even when the reader is skimming.

For most designs, a few vertical alignments are enough. For example, all headings and basic text in a book might align to the left margin, and both poetry and block quotes will also be left-aligned, but to a place that's a third of an inch or so from the margin line. This means there are two vertical alignments: one for all the main text and one for all the block quotes and poetry (see Figure 7).

The fewer alignments you use, the neater a design will look. The more alignments you use, the more eclectic it will look. Having various alignments works for certain projects, especially dynamic posters or flyers, but multipage documents with lots of text are better served with just a few alignments.

Horizontal Alignment

Vertical alignment is often the first type of alignment new designers think about, but don't forget horizontal alignment. Lining elements up both horizontally and vertically increases a design's tidiness and creates more opportunities to guide viewers' eyes.

For example, in a (square) Instagram post highlighting a rectangular image, you can align accompanying text with the top of the image (see Figure 8). The top of the image provides a strong horizontal line, so aligning the text with that line makes it easy for viewers' eyes to go directly from the image to the text that talks about it.

Horizontal alignment is especially important when pages or panels are meant to be viewed at the same time but are designed separately. This can happen with printed book spreads (where you may see only one page at a time on the computer), pamphlets, and other similar designs. In cases like this, keep track of where elements begin and end on each page so those elements will line up in the final printed product. Specialized

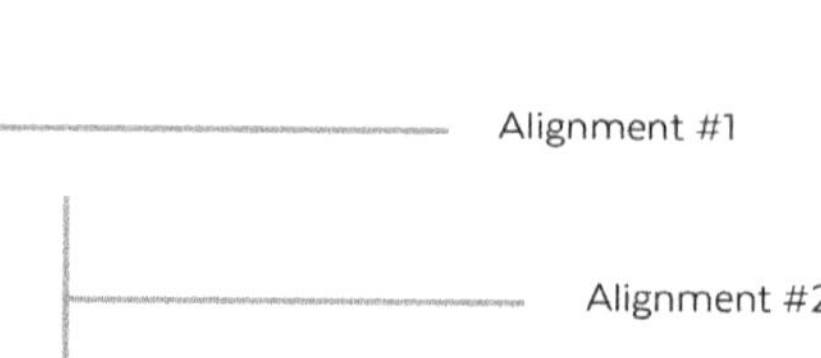

Chapter Title

Obitate post que nem voluptat ipsus, consed excepta tecerfe rchilis maio blam vel inverae. Ehenda quam nem quam quias a nat ex eicimos ut elibusandus rero et faciet maxime remquid quatem endit ut utetur aspellaccus.

Coneturis vel inime ped eicia que ni tem re disto eum si ommos cumquia sinimagnihic tem exceste nihil excest pa quam voluptaquo eossi berspe ex et veliquuntio volupta tenditi iscium que la consequ idemporum utem suntibea vel molupta tempor si rerum fugia dolupta nonsequis sa inimi, suntes rehent.

Heading Level 1

Ressinc tatur? Qui abore pellore rereped quas volectios et opturerrum eius, exerum doluptate et rem ides nonse re lab il ium ra veliquae venisit, culparc ipsuntecus cus.

> This is a block quote. Lestium hilitae essimus aria perovidel idel iniet magnia excesti cusam, quasincta nonseque nos con repuda simet fugitia ssintur, coreic.

To qui ipid qui dunt mil et acipsam sus nonserumet ut alignatqui odipicid moloressunto bla duntiur, cor simet vero molorporibus dolorioriam, sa volorestia si deni dolupti nonsed et vernatectam, qui qui dolor ma duciam re nost, vid ma voloria escimus, si nobis ut il molo omnis et lauda cuptate vel idesed mo dolupta volupta temquae. Occupti aspici unt omnistrum sinctis quuntibus modia

Figure 7. This page has two main vertical alignments: one for the title, heading, and main text, and one for block quotes. (There's also a sneaky third alignment for the paragraph indents in the main text.) Fonts used: Core Paint, Core Paint B1, Minion Pro, and Texta Regular.

design software usually has options to manage these elements' placement automatically.

Aligning with Curves

Curves present a common alignment problem. It's difficult to align a straight line—like a capital *L* or a left-aligned block of text—with the outer edge of a circle, ellipse, or other curve. If a designer places the long stem of an *L* against a line and then places a circle against that same line above it, the *L* has a large amount of surface area touching that line,

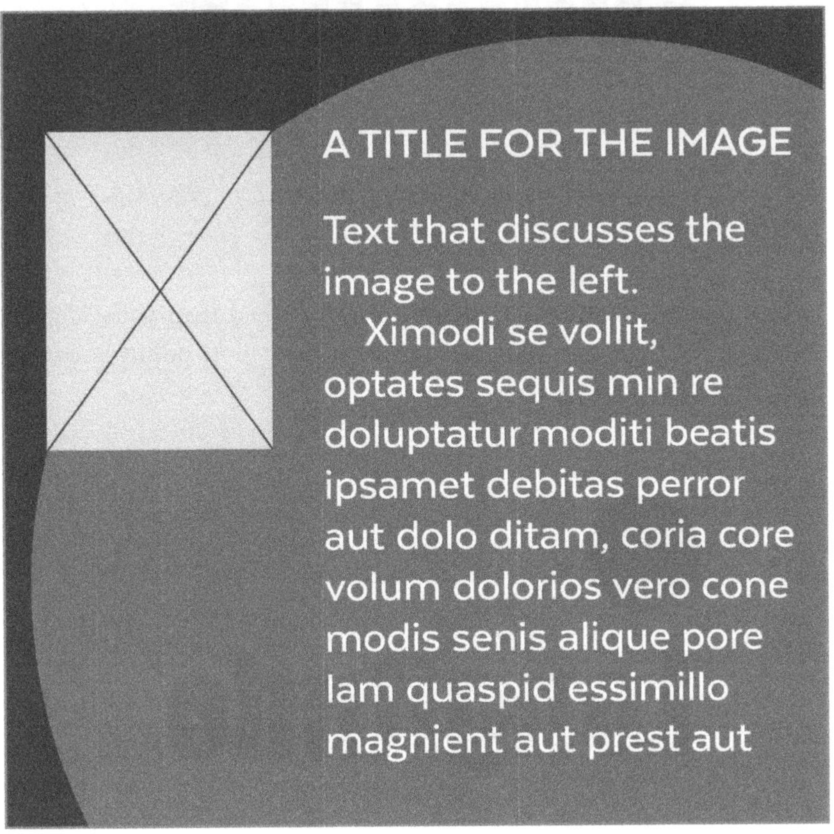

Figure 8. The top of the placeholder image on the left aligns with the top of the title text to the right. This reinforces that the image and text are related, and viewers easily slide from the image to the text. Font used: Texta.

while the circle has only one point of contact. This creates the illusion that the two things aren't aligned with each other.

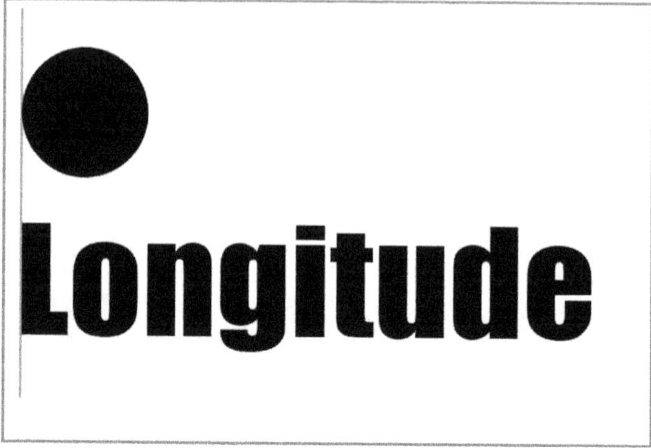

Figure 9. The outer edge of the circle and the stem of the L are aligned, but the circle looks like it's farther to the right. Font used: Impact.

In instances like these, it's better to *look* aligned than to *be* aligned. Nudging the circle over to the left makes it share more points of contact with the original line.

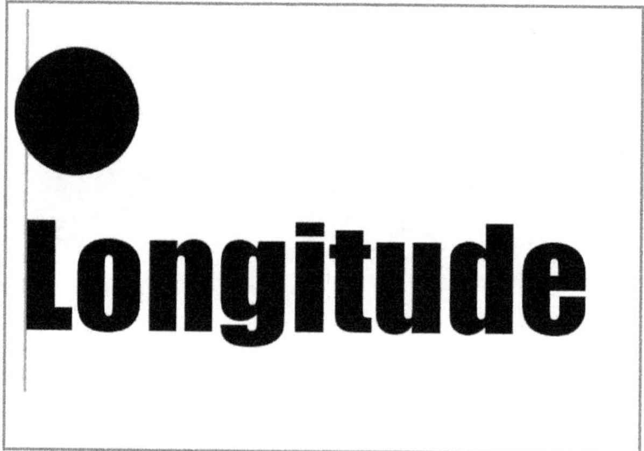

Figure 10. Allow the curve to have more contact with the aligning line.

The amount of adjustment necessary varies, and sometimes it's more appropriate to align the strong line (in Figure 10, the stem of the *L*) with the center of the circle.

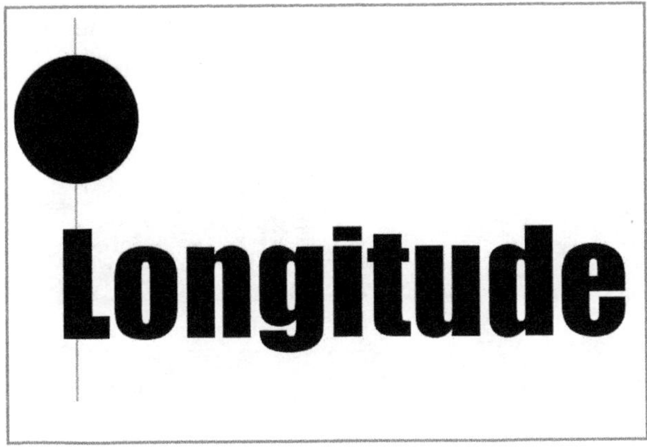

Figure 11. Sometimes center alignment is the only way to win.

This nudging happens even within typefaces. Many geometric typefaces (those in which the *O* is almost a perfect circle) and typefaces with very pointy *W*'s and *V*'s have the pointed and curved letters extend below the baseline. This gives the letters more points of contact with the baseline, so they look aligned with the surrounding letters. Because graphic design is about visual appeal and functionality rather than mathematics, looking aligned is far more important than being aligned.

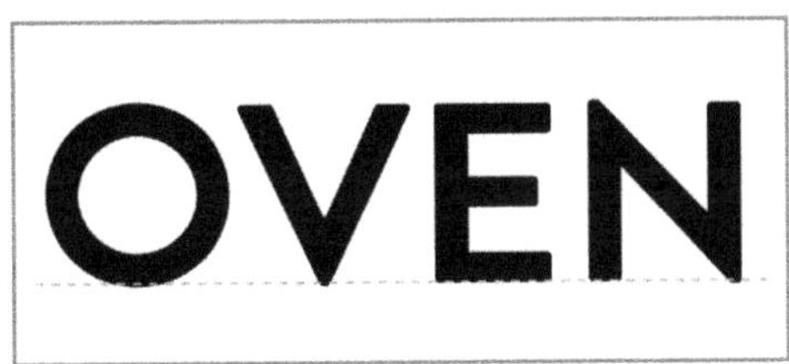

Figure 12. The curve of the O *and the points of the* V *and* N *extend beyond the dotted baseline. This increases the surface area of the letter that touches the line. The* E *has a flat base and looks aligned when it's flush with the baseline. Font used: Brandon Grotesque Bold.*

Eyeline Alignment

If you use an image with a human or animal whose face or eyes are visible, be aware of where it's looking. For example, if the face-having subject looks directly to one side, that's a powerful opportunity. Most viewers will want to see what the subject is looking at. Don't ignore a powerful eyeline like this. Instead, lean into it for dramatic effect.

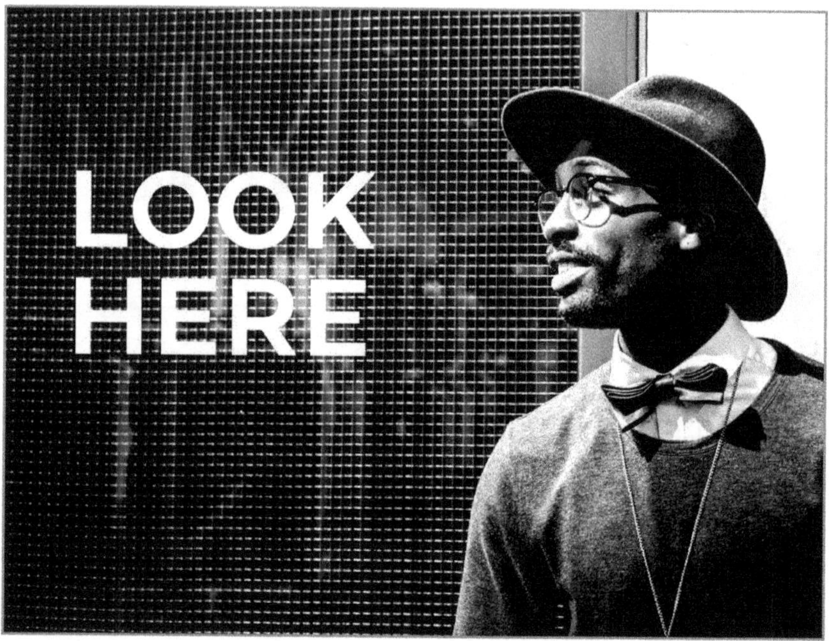

Figure 13. The model is clearly looking at something to the left side of the design, creating a great location for important stuff! Font used: Texta Heavy. Public-domain image from Nappy.co.

Alignment Misfires

When you're in diagnosis mode on a weak design, check to see if everything on the design is aligned with something. Usually, each element should align with some other element, either vertically or horizontally. This helps everything look tidy and intentional.

Additionally, avoid having large chunks of text center aligned. Although center-aligned text looks balanced on a page, each line starts at a different horizontal point, so it's harder for readers to find the beginning of each line. This isn't a huge problem for short chunks of text like titles or pull quotes, but text you want folks to read at length should have a left alignment for them to return to at the beginning of each line.

This text is centered, so the beginning of each line is in a different place. This makes it a poor choice for long chunks of text because readers have to constantly find the new place to start.

This text is left aligned, so every line starts in the same place. This means readers can get in a rhythm where they reach the end of a line and snap back to the same starting place every single time. It's a better choice for long chunks of text you want folks to read carefully.

Figure 14. Choose left-aligned text for large chunks of text you want folks to read carefully. This text is left-aligned, so every line starts at the same place and readers can get into a steady rhythm. Font used: Minion Pro.

Proximity

Alignment is primarily about where a designer puts elements on a page, and so is **proximity**. The principle of proximity dictates that the closer two things are to each other, the more logically related they are (the inverse is also true). By carefully controlling the distances between elements, designers articulate how closely related those elements are.

Proximity is one of the most subtly powerful organization tools in a designer's toolkit. Even if you use the same alignment, typeface, size, and color for everything, you can calibrate proximity to organize even complex documents.

Consider a long, nonfiction project with chapter breaks and two levels of heading (Figure 15). Even without changing type size or style, you can create a visual flow.

1. **Start the chapters on a new page.** This creates a dramatic spatial break between the previous chapter and the new one.
2. **Leave two or more lines of space above the first level of heading and one line of space below it.** This spacing setup clearly indicates that the heading belongs with what comes after it rather than what comes before it.
3. **Leave one or two lines of space above the second level of heading and no space below it.** This sends a similar signal—that the heading is related to what follows it, not what comes before—but because the space involved is smaller, the heading seems less important than the first-level heading.

Um ulparum voluptas aut eos volores aut velignatate nos ipsaperum fugia non coria expernati necabo. Bus doluptat quos aut ati si tempe por alis et, comni con reculpa natiae prepell uptatem nusam qui nem ulpa volut eruptatium nectore, ut lacepud aepudit ex estionsequi id uteseque essin nulparunt aborumq uatur? Quiduci assequi simincto dolorum quidunda ipsant, quisima as eaquatetus pres nonseris plabore nditatur?

Heading Level 2

Bea eatusaerum nonsedi vellabo. Apelia deles aliquam venis miniate ipsum facea sed quo ea volore officius audae oditatquia adit offic totate plaboribus aut at volut apidere provid quidus.

Ex etur, sequam asit rempe nonecaborem. Nam as dolupta tempore rem voluptur, omnimaio cum duciliquiam fugiam rerument, seque dem. Hictatiae dis plitass equistoria es dolecep taturemporum eum in eatias elicius quo volupti cullis sam quos nimos earuptur solupta ni doluptis volenist escipit atiatur, odissedit atem volestes eat et quo blandae velicatem fugia sunt landucius moditiore dia duciisi nvendis nimilla simposs imolupta in ped est volecat.

Chapter Title

Obitate post que nem voluptat ipsus, consed excepta tecerferchilis maio blam vel inverae. Ehenda quam nem quam quias a nat ex eicimos ut elibusandus rero et faciet maxime remquid quatem endit ut utetur aspellaccus.

Coneturis vel inime ped eicia que ni tem re disto eum si ommos cumquia sinimagnihic tem exceste nihil excest pa quam voluptaquo eossi berspe ex et veliquuntio volupta tenditi iscium que la consequ idemporum utem suntibea vel molupta tempor si rerum fugia dolupta nonsequis sa inimi, suntes rehent.

Heading Level 1

Ressinc tatur? Qui abore pellore rereped quas volectios et opturerrum eius, exerum doluptate et rem ides nonse re lab il ium ra veliquae venisit, culparc ipsuntecus cus.

Lestium hilitae essimus aria perovidel idel iniet magnia excesti cusam, quasincta nonseque nos con repuda simet fugitia ssintur, coreic.

Heading Level 2

To qui ipid qui dunt mil et acipsam sus nonserumet ut alignatqui odipicid moloressunto bla duntiur, cor simet vero molorporibus dolorioriam, sa volorestia si deni dolupti nonsed et vernatectam, qui qui dolor ma duciam re nost, vid ma voloria escimus, si nobis ut il molo omnis et lauda cuptate vel idesed mo dolupta volupta

Figure 15. Even with extreme restrictions on other design principles, proximity can organize elements on a page in a way that communicates your intention.

A designer could further strengthen this structure by putting the chapter title or first-level heading in all caps, a different size, a different typeface, or a different type style. But even without those tools, proximity alone creates an organized skeleton. If you ever find yourself designing within very constricting parameters, look to proximity first.

A useful exercise for practicing proximity is what I (creatively) call the Dot Game. Get a series of circles—either of paper or in a computer program—that are all the same. Same color, same size, same everything. Then try to change their proximity to each other to communicate abstract concepts or tell stories. Unity. Exclusion. Friendship. *Romeo & Juliet.* Go wild.

The results of Dot Game exercises won't be perfect, but they help designers think more intentionally about how to place objects in their designs to reinforce and support specific messages.

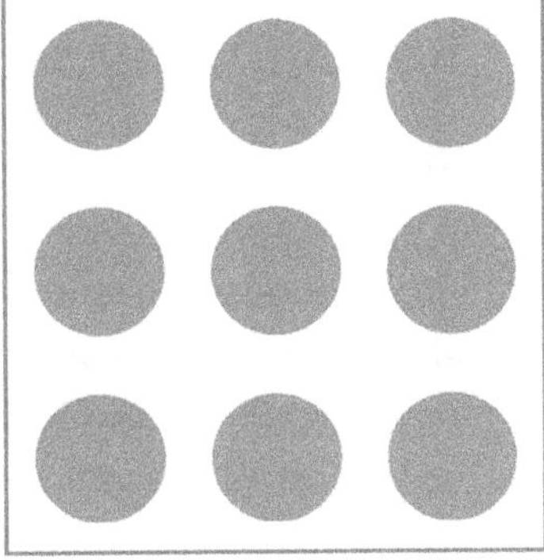

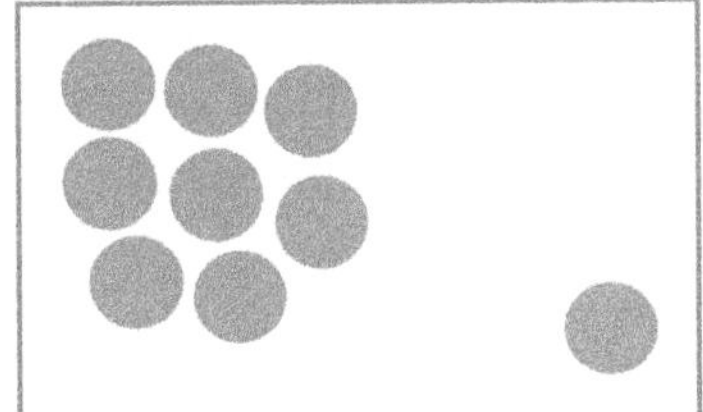

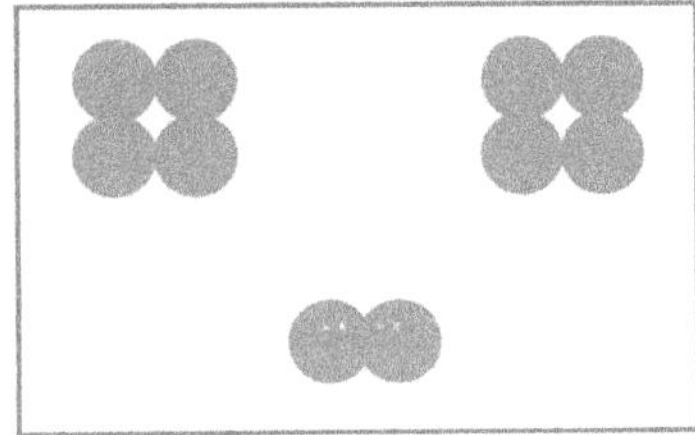

Figure 16 (top). Unity

Figure 17 (center). Exclusion

Figure 18 (bottom). Romeo & Juliet

Proximity Misfires

Proximity mishaps take many forms, but some of the most common ones I see involve headings. One problem involves setting headings with the same space above them as they have below. This is especially common in web design when folks use off-the-shelf styles and templates without the know-how to adjust them. But this sort of spacing can make it unclear whether readers are looking at a pull quote (or other flavor text) or at an actual organizing signal. As noted previously, headings should always be closer to the text that follows them than the text that precedes them.

Another issue is setting body text closer to headings than to other body text paragraphs. Again, this is more common online, where space between paragraphs is the most common new-paragraph signal. (Books and other long-form printed works tend to use indents at the beginning of each paragraph instead.) Body text paragraphs are always most logically related and should be closer to each other than they are to headings.

Building Hierarchy

The four basic principles of design should serve each project's message, purpose, and audience. Just as no grammar or usage rule is appropriate in all contexts, there is no one right way to employ contrast, repetition, alignment, and proximity. One concept that you can use to help guide how you use the four basics is **hierarchy**.

A design's hierarchy refers to the order of importance for the content. The top of the hierarchy is whatever you want the viewer to see first, the second item on the hierarchy is the thing you want them to see next, and so on. Here are some examples of elements that might go at the top of a design hierarchy:

- The title on a book cover
- The professional's name on a business card
- An attractive photo with a strong focal point on a flyer or ad
- A restaurant name on a mailable menu

But for each of these examples, a different element might go at the top of the hierarchy depending on the purpose and message of the piece. Maybe a moody title with the word *grave* in it is the best way to attract an audience interested in a book with necromancers in it, but the author's name might be a better draw for a book by a well-known author, and a richly detailed illustration or emotional photograph might be better at attracting an audience looking for a particular tone. Similarly, a business card *might* emphasize the person the most, but for some businesses, it is more important to emphasize the work they do, the problems they solve, or their company name. Pick the top of the hierarchy based on which element best communicates each project's message.

The last item in the hierarchy—the very last thing the viewer will see—is almost as important as the top of the hierarchy. This is the visual grammar equivalent of end emphasis. Just as the end of a sentence can linger in a reader's mind, the last thing on a visual hierarchy should be something the designer wants them to retain. On one-page items, this is usually a call to action: visit this website; contact this person; show up at this place and time. On a business card, for example, the bottom of the hierarchy will almost always be the contact information for the person handing out the card.

To put an element at the top of a layout's hierarchy, designers give it the strongest contrast of any element in the design. It should be visually loud, usually with multiple types of contrast layered on top of it: size, color, etc. The contrast gets audiences to look at this element first, or at least to get there quickly.

To use the eyeline alignment example from earlier, there are two places a viewer might look first. They might see *Look Here* first, because it's white against a dark background (value contrast), and the strokes of the letters are thick, which contrasts with the fine detail of the background (size contrast). But some viewers look at faces first if a design has them, so tracing the man's eyeline to point to the top of the hierarchy helps catch those viewers and guide them to the headline.

From the top of the hierarchy, you can continue to use (subtler) contrasts to guide viewers to the next element in a design, but you can also use repetition, alignment, and proximity. If the viewer hits the headline and there's something aligned with it just below, their eyes will drop down to it, especially if the color or typeface is repeated (see Figure 19). Proximity can help viewers get from one lesser paragraph to another before sliding down to a call to action.

For hierarchy to work, it's important to (1) make conscious choices about what is most important, (2) start at the top with the focal point, (3) be brave about contrast, and (4) keep it as simple as possible. If there are too many things a viewer needs to look at, the design might have too many messages in it. If that's the case, strip elements out to simplify.

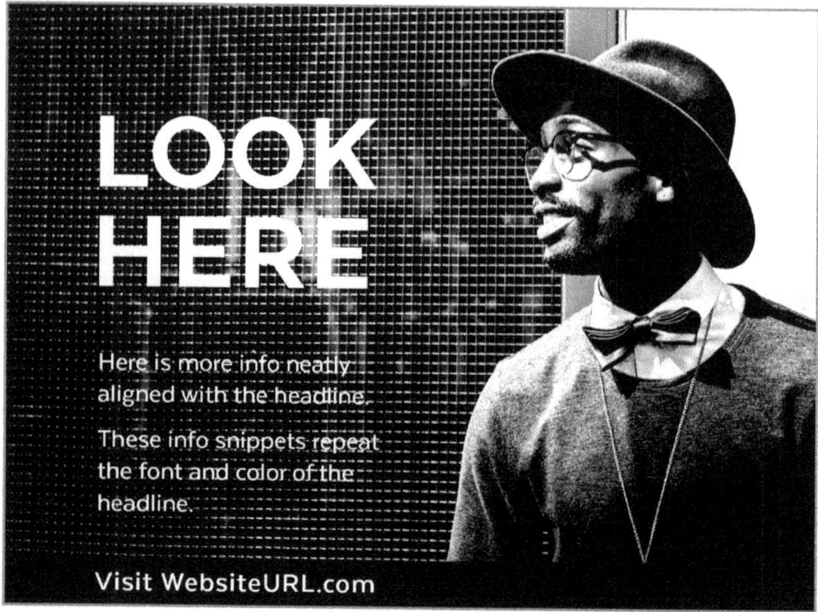

Figure 19. This ad template uses high contrast on the headline, a repeated font family, a strong left alignment for the text, and tidy proximity that separates the text into distinct groups.

Working with Type

As editors, our forays into design are more likely to be heavier on text than on imagery. This makes choosing and setting type one of our most important design skills. When selecting a typeface and setting it on a page, there are three main considerations: personality, legibility, and readability. The first two (personality and legibility) relate to the typeface you choose; the last (readability) has more to do with how you set type on the page. All of them impact how effectively your design communicates.

Choosing a Typeface

When choosing a typeface, consider the tone and the purpose of the design. Should it be more playful or more elegant? Will the words be printed large (like on a poster) or small (like on a business card)? Is the intended audience made up of young readers or more experienced adults?

These sorts of questions help you decide how much personality and legibility you need. Personality and legibility aren't necessarily opposite ends of a spectrum, but often the typefaces with more pizzazz are less legible, especially at smaller sizes. Be aware of your project's needs so you can find the right balance between personality features and legibility.

Personality

When assessing a typeface's personality, designers can use the *Jagen* test, as described by Jo Mackiewicz. This involves setting the word *Jagen* in a typeface to see many of its core features.[1] *Jagen* highlights many of the telltale features of a typeface, including (but not limited to) the following:

- Whether some capital letters extend below the baseline (like the *J* in Minion Pro)
- If the lowercase *g*'s and *a*'s are double- or single-story (Acumin, Modern No. 20, Montserrat, Minion Pro, and Poor Richard have double-story *a*'s; Modern No. 20, Minion Pro, and Poor Richard have double-story *g*'s)
- How the stems of lowercase *n*'s appear (usually lowercase *r*'s will be similar)
- How the most-used letter in the English language (*e*) displays
- How much height difference the uppercase and lowercase letters have
- How thick and thin the extremes of the letterforms are (the thin parts of Modern No. 20 are very thin and the thick parts are very thick, whereas Montauk's letter strokes are the same width throughout)
- How wide or narrow the letters are.

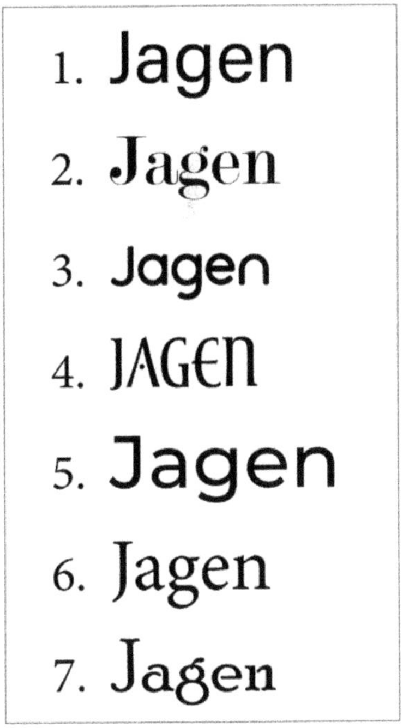

1. Jagen
2. Jagen
3. Jagen
4. JAGEN
5. Jagen
6. Jagen
7. Jagen

Figure 20. Jagen displays for (1) Acumin Pro Regular, (2) Modern No. 20, (3) Montauk, (4) P22 Monumental Titling, (5) Montserrat Medium, (6) Minion Pro Regular, and (7) Poor Richard.

---

1 Jo Mackiewicz, "How to Use Five Letterforms to Gauge a Typeface's Personality: A Research-Driven Method." *Journal of Technical Writing and Communication*, vol. 35(3), 291–315, 2005.

In addition to the features above, there are some typeface features (identified by Mackiewicz) that make a font seem friendlier or more professional.

Friendlier typefaces tend to:

- Have imperfections (there are gaps in the lowercase *g*'s in many "handwritten" typefaces, for example),
- Be simpler, and
- Have more roundness to their letterforms.[2]

More professional typefaces usually have:

- Balanced terminals (for example, Minion Pro has rigid lines on its serifs, but those are balanced by curves that lead from the stem to the serifs),
- Moderate thick-to-thin transitions (Modern No. 20 has pronounced thick-to-thin transition; Montauk has no thick-to-thin transition; Minion Pro has a moderate thick-to-thin transition),
- A moderate weight (usually the regular version of a typeface, not the thin or bold version), and
- Have moderate proportion.[3]

Proportion is a measure of the ratio between uppercase and lowercase letters in a typeface. For some typefaces, like P22 Monumental Titling, the ratio is 1:1, so the lowercase letters are just as tall as the uppercase ones. Other typefaces, like Poor Richard, have such a low x-height (that is, the lowercase letters are very short) that the ratio of uppercase letters to lowercase ones is closer to 1:2. Most typefaces fall somewhere between those two extremes, with moderate proportions falling somewhere around 2:3 (as in Times New Roman).

Legibility

Legibility refers to how easy it is to distinguish one letterform from another in the same typeface. Proportion is very important when

2 Mackiewicz, 301–304.
3 Mackiewicz, 305–309.

determining legibility—a moderate proportion means the lowercase letters aren't too small to see but are still different enough from uppercase letters that they're easy to distinguish. So when you're aiming for legibility, look for a moderate x-height, low-to-moderate thick-to-thin transitions, and fully formed letters.

When analyzing a typeface for legibility, designers often use some test text (also known as "placeholder" or "dummy" text) to set in each typeface. If you're designing before you have finalized text for a project, you can use various forms of **lorem ipsum**, a design term for random (often Latin) text. Some programs (like Adobe InDesign) generate placeholder text for you, but I also enjoy placeholder text that makes me laugh (like Cheese Ipsum[4]).

Tried-and-True Typefaces

If you're in a hurry or if the vast world of typefaces is intimidating, there's no shame in relying on some tried-and-true typefaces that get the job done. Below are a few solid serif typefaces for basic body text and sans serif typefaces for headings. Remember that, for main body text, serif fonts are more common in print (and for ebooks) and sans serif fonts are more common online. In print, it often looks good to have sans serif headings paired with serif body text. The inverse is true online, though it's also common to use the same sans serif typeface for both headings and body text.

Serif Typefaces

- Caslon. This typeface is highly readable and has some warm, homey notes to it.
- Garamond. This is a popular typeface for books. It tends to read a bit smaller than some typefaces, so if you're designing for audiences who are likely to need reading glasses, increase the size a bit.
- Jenson. This readable typeface has a "classic" personality.
- Minion. This is the default typeface for most Adobe programs, and for good reason. It's moderate in most of its features and hits a lot of legibility sweet spots.

4 http://www.cheeseipsum.co.uk

- Palatino. This common typeface for books has letterforms that are a bit wider than some other entries on this list, which can make it seem a bit looser and friendlier while still solidly professional.
- Alegreya. This readable typeface is a great choice when you don't have access to one of the previously listed options and you need a free alternative. It's available in a variety of weights and has open-source licensing.[5]

Sans Serif Typefaces

- Helvetica. This typeface is a bit overused, but deservedly so. It's carefully crafted to be balanced and readable at large sizes, making it an excellent choice for headings and signage.
- Futura. This is a popular typeface for online publications, but it was originally designed for (and is effective in) print.
- Brandon Grotesque. This typeface falls a bit more on the friendly side of the friendly–professional spectrum, but it is still legible and workable for many professional contexts.
- Optima. This typeface feels a lot like (and is commonly mistaken for) a serif typeface, as it has a slight flare at the ends of some letterforms and more thick-to-thin transition than many common sans serif fonts.
- Alegreya Sans. This is the sans serif, open-source companion to Alegreya. It comes in a variety of weights and is free to use. Alegreya Sans is a strong option for body text as well as for headings.

Setting the Type

The final consideration for a text-heavy design like a book or an article-heavy website is the typesetting. Typesetting affects the readability of the text—that is, how easy it is to read the text for a long time and retain information from it.

The most important consideration for readable typesetting is line length. Ideally, text that will be read at length should have 45 to 75 characters per line on average. For younger readers or for text set in

5 Google Fonts (fonts.google.com) and Font Squirrel (fontsquirrel.com), two excellent resources for free fonts, both have Alegreya.

multiple columns, steer closer to the lower end of the range. For denser texts, closer to 75 characters per line is fine. All other requirements being equal, I usually prefer to keep average line lengths in the mid-60s. Overly long lines make it difficult to retain information, while overly short lines feel choppy after more than a brief paragraph.

The other major consideration for most designs is whether to align the text with a ragged right edge (that is, left-aligned text) or to justify the text so both the left and right edges are a straight line.

A ragged right edge is usually better for variable contexts, like web pages, and for narrow columns. In narrow columns, justified text will often have large spaces between words to keep the column edges straight. (And since online readers encounter your design on screens ranging from smartphones to large desktop monitors, you can't always control how wide their columns are.) These spaces can be distracting, and it's often better to let the lines break more freely.

Justified text is better for nonvariable contexts, like printed books, because designers can control the line length and word spacing better. The neat vertical lines on either side of the text block keep everything tidy and sorted, and readers can get in a steady rhythm for where lines begin and end. The last line of a left-justified paragraph should remain aligned to the left, not stretched across the entire line (most software will do this for you automatically).

Conclusion

Foundational design principles, hierarchy, and typography are solid building blocks for the grammar of visual rhetoric. But just as with written language, nothing beats practice. So break out your template for editorial letters, your business card, or your blog, and test out your (visual) grammar skills!

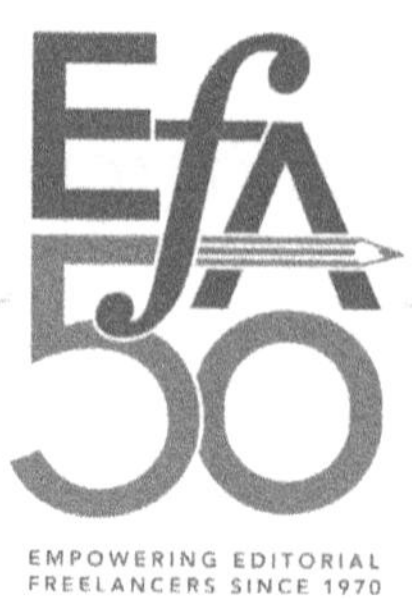

About the Editorial Freelancers Association (EFA)

Celebrating 50 Years!
Dedicated to the Education and Growth of Editorial Freelancers

The EFA is a national not-for-profit — 501(c)6 — organization, headquartered in New York City, run by member volunteers, all of whom are also freelancers. The EFA's members, experienced in a wide range of professional skills, live and work all across the United States and in other countries.

A pioneer in organizing freelancers into a network for mutual support and advancement, the EFA is now recognized throughout the publishing industry as the source for professional editorial assistance.

We welcome people of every race, color, culture, religion or no religion, gender identity, gender expression, age, national or ethnic origin, ancestry, citizenship, education, ability, health, neurotype, marital/parental status, socio-economic background, sexual orientation, and/or military status. We are nothing without our members, and encourage everyone to volunteer and to participate in our community.

The EFA sells a variety of specialized booklets, not unlike this one, on topics of interest to editorial freelancers at the-efa.org.

The EFA hosts online, asynchronous courses, real-time webinars, and on-demand recorded webinars designed especially for freelance editors, writers, and other editorial specialists around the world. You can learn more about our Education Program at the-efa.org.

To learn about these and other EFA offerings, visit the-efa.org and join us on social media:

Twitter: @EFAFreelancers
Instagram: @efa_editors
Facebook: editorialfreelancersassociation
LinkedIn: editorial-freelancers

www.ingramcontent.com/pod-product-compliance
Ingram Content Group UK Ltd.
Pitfield, Milton Keynes, MK11 3LW, UK
UKHW020421250726
13967UKWH00007B/2755